# the extended christian family

# toward the extended christian family

### edited by Paul F. Wilczak, Ph.D.

ABBEY PRESS
St. Meinrad, Indiana 47577

The five chapters of this book originally appeared as articles in the *Focus* series, "Toward the Extended Christian Family," published in the February 1980 through June 1980 issues of *MARRIAGE and Family Living* magazine. They are here copyrighted as a collection in slightly revised form.

PHOTO CREDITS: Alan Cliburn, Cover; James Shaffer, pages 6 and 44 & 45; Robert Eckert, page 10; Mimi Forsyth, page 20; H. Armstrong Roberts, page 30; Jim Whitmer, page 53; Bob Taylor, page 54; Evelin Sanders, page 61.

Library of Congress Card Number
80-69137
ISBN 0-87029-170-X

# CONTENTS

# Introduction

We are living in what has been called the age of the nuclear family. Sociologists and anthropologists have observed our patterns of life and noted that the family today exists in smaller groups. Parents and children tend to live together as units apart. Their households are separate from those of relatives. The extended family household in which I lived as a child is becoming much less common. Our home included two grandparents, two uncles, two aunts, and a cousin. There was a lot of daily social activity around the dinner table.

Today's pattern is different. Parent(s) plus off-spring households have become the rule. This has, in fact, been a partial realization of the American dream of "a man's home is his castle." Castles possess thick walls, however, and deep moats. They are insulated territories, safe from outsiders, except for carefully regulated contacts.

Such insulation has had its effect on the church as well. Instead of sprawling across a neighborhood of people in close, daily contact, the church occupies a nice, tidy corner. Church members often have their only meetings with other members of the congregation at Sunday services in the church building. The communal meal aspect of the Eucharist, which was a symbolic deepening of an everyday social value, has become a substitute for ordinary communal meals, which now rarely occur.

The isolating effect of contemporary patterns of living has transformed churches from communities of extended families into social institutions. This means that the people who go to church are united more by common observances than by a common life. Perhaps the growth of religious orders in the Roman Catholic Church in the decades before Vatican II was a reaction to the beginning of this isolating trend. Perhaps it seemed that community life was possible only in convents, monasteries, and religious houses.

This book deals with another possibility—that the local church itself can be transformed into an extended Christian family. Such a possibility does not imply giving up private property and moving into large communal dwellings. But it does mean taking to heart the directive of Jesus, "Love one another, as I have loved you." And it also means working in everyday life toward the goal expressed in Christ's prayer, "That they all may be one."

The authors of the chapters are Bishop John J. Sullivan and staff members of the Center for Pastoral Life and Ministry which he established in the Roman Catholic Diocese of Kansas City-St. Joseph, Missouri. In a profound sense, the work of the Center is directed toward facilitating the growth of the extended Christian family. This is done by under-standing ministry as derived from baptism, and then training baptized persons to realize their ministerial responsibilities.

Chapter One begins with an overview by Bishop Sullivan. His perspective is developed in the rest of the book with chapters by Dr. Margot K. Hover (on family ministry to elderly "partners"), by Dr. Paul F. Wilczak (on listening as ministry), by Sr. Susan Rakoczy (on social consciousness and the family), and by Ms. Maureen Kelly (on family initiation rituals and conversion). We hope you find our efforts interesting, helpful, and challenging.

*Paul F. Wilczak*

# I
# My Vision of the Parish as a Family of Families

## by Most Rev. John J. Sullivan

*The Bishop of the Roman Catholic Diocese of Kansas City-St. Joseph, Missouri, John J. Sullivan is a native of Oklahoma. He is a graduate of St. Benedict's College in Atchison, Kansas, and Kenrick Seminary in St. Louis, Missouri. He was formerly Bishop of the Diocese of Grand Island, Nebraska.*

Some psychologists say dreams fulfill our wishes. If that is true, my dreams reveal a wish that people of all ages — children, young couples, older parents, grandparents, single persons — be taken up into the genuine joy that comes with responding to our Lord. It is the joy that can smile through the tears, a touch of blessedness that takes us beyond our confines and disappointments. These are my dreams, my wishes, but there are days when an old man's dreams seem to vanish with the morning light, days when I pray at Mass, "I can only dream, Lord. The work is yours alone." But our Lord somehow lets me know we need to work together — we all need to work together with him. And that too is the image of my dream.

In Chapter Two of the Acts of the Apostles, St. Peter speaks of young persons having visions and old men dreaming dreams. I spoke my dream to some younger persons and they seemed to be able to envision it as a reality. How can a dream become real? What is really in a dream? I dream of people, young and old, taken up, responding, working together with our Lord. It is like the family of God, people connected in and through and with him.

Yet when morning breaks upon this world which I see each day in my pastoral work, a different picture meets my eyes. I catch sight of many lonely people, people in need of ministry, people who seemingly cannot be reached. "How many, O Lord, are out there? Can I leave them up to you?" I see them at worship, in the streets, strangers to me, strangers to each other, perhaps even strangers in their own families. How many times people have come with their troubles, their guilt, their anguish and said, "Father, I just don't understand my spouse, my children, my parents. We don't talk the same language. It's like living with a stranger!" When I reflect upon their words, sometimes the image of the tower of Babel from the book of Genesis meets my mind's eye — a picture of words isolating people more and more. But sometimes a different light also flickers, bright tongues of fire, strangers speaking in alien languages yet understanding one another and marveling. Dreams and visions of redemption, but dreams with meaning for today.

In the Pentecost story from St. Luke, a wonderful transformation is described. The talk that separates people becomes the witness uniting them. And the more I reflect on my experience with people, the more I am convinced that giving witness is always what unites them. So perhaps my dream is really of people giving witness out of the wondrous power of the spirit of God. Giving witness seems to be where my dream is at, and that makes it a dream of shared

13

ministry, for giving witness is what ministry is about.

Theologians sometimes speak of bishops as having the "fullness of the priesthood." This brings with it, for me as a bishop, a sense of full responsibility for giving witness in my diocese. In doing this, any ability I possess comes from God but choosing the response is up to me. I feel called to serve the people of the Diocese of Kansas City-St. Joseph, and through them the entire Church. Yet I cannot reach all those people. I ordain and delegate priests and deacons and commission religious to help me and to share in this ministry. And yet we still are too few in number to meet the needs of the people.

We give public witness to our people and to all others around us. But more importantly, we give witness *with* the people. Giving witness is the vocation of every Christian. Baptism into the death and resurrection of Christ goes to the very core of a person. It calls us out of a purely human existence and into a living of the Christian life. This makes sense only as personal witness to the redemptive presence of God. Of course the Christian life is not "heaven on earth," and we surely don't lead it because it feels so good. There's no denying that at times it involves the mystery of suffering. But in spite of this we all comprehend the presence of some immense value in our Christian way of life: the reality of God in the many twists, turns, and reverses we experience. To that reality we are called to give witness through our lives.

But what really is giving witness? For now, let me call it "making a faithful response to the presence of God in strangers." In more ordinary language, it is letting God introduce us to the other members of his family. In this way we can discover that deep down we're not strangers after all. And I dream of doing everything I can to help this happen.

Sometimes I wonder, "What is my role?" I reflect on my dream of God's family sharing the responsibility of giving witness, and another question arises. How are people to be helped to meet their responsibility and call to give witness? They say to me, "Bishop, we just don't know how to witness. Ministry is too important to leave to people like us who don't know what they're doing." When I hear that, I am tempted to say, "God will provide." And he has!

God wills that we all be given a chance to grow and learn and do his will. People need to be prepared to meet the ministerial responsibilities of giving the witness expected of them. Such preparation will begin to transform the lonely crowd of strangers into the family of God. It can mean people reaching out and being reached out to in a new way in the Church.

Witnessing cannot be accomplished by bishops, priests, deacons, and religious alone. Our monopolizing of this responsibility may have seemed to be the case in the Catholic Church in the past. An immigrant church found a heavy reliance on clerics and religious unavoidable in laying the foundation for the task ahead. Today, as a result, there are more educated lay persons in the church than ever before. They form a mature, accomplished people. They are ready, as the First Epistle of St. Peter puts it, to be transformed into the "living stones" of the renewed church which will rise above those foundations. In this renewal the "new way" will complement and fulfill the "old." And this too is my dream.

At the exchange of peace during Mass, Catholics greet one another with the words, "The peace of Christ be with you." It is in this gesture of Christian friendship that the merger of "old" and "new" are expressed. The priest and deacon have just encouraged the people to turn to one another in recognition and love. It is this affirmation and its deep Christian meaning that must now be carried out of the church building and into the communities where the living Church is built. In large parishes today, it is common to turn to a neighbor and not know that person. It is easy to feel like a stranger among strangers when this happens over and over. But "the Church where people live" is the group of Church members living within a neighborhood. This cluster of Christian families is an important part of my dream. There, in a group of families, people can experience the Church on a truly livable and personally meaningful scale. They can learn to know one another in Christ because they will find it possible to know each other in a human sense. There too, and on this personal level, I feel, the needs of people must be ministered to by the Church. I consider this a pastoral responsibility.

But ministry, on all levels, requires skill. And skill comes from training and experience. Some Catholics hearing the call to ministry fear that they "won't know what they're doing." This must become their challenge to grow. The dream can become real and practical only if the opportunity to grow and to develop the necessary skills is provided. And this is why my dream includes the Center for Pastoral Life and Ministry.

The Center is a group of professional people who have formed a team to train ministers in our diocese. They are professionals in religious education, Scripture, family ministry, administration, theology, spirituality, and pastoral marriage counseling who can develop training programs in cooperation with parish staff persons. The articles in this book are written by staff members of the Center and will reveal some of their work in progress and already completed. I believe such commitment to provide excellent training for ministry is vital to the future of the Church. The goodwill and responsive intentions of the people need to be formed and raised to the level of real ministerial competence. Such formation will renew our traditional Christian values by emphasizing their relevance to life. And this can happen only in the parishes where the faith is lived by ordinary people. For ministry or giving witness to the faith takes place only on the local level where people meet face to face. There all dreams of redemption are tested by reality.

At the Center an understanding of ministry has been developed which expresses the structure of my dream and the content of my hope for the future. This understanding includes five points.

First, ministry is pastoral or centered in a local church under the care of a pastor. This is fitting, for the pastor symbolizes the unity of all ministries and their orientation to Christ, our principal pastor.

Second, pastoral ministry is service. This means meeting the real needs of other people. Their benefit and good becomes a major goal. But the means to reach the goal also becomes a giving of self. Service is not a job but a gift of one's own person.

Ministerial service, however, is motivated by love and faith. This third characteristic points beyond humanism. Service itself is an act of love, loving one's neighbor as one's self. But such love is founded in commitment, through faith, to the great commandment to love God. We love the human persons we can see because that is the only way we can truly express our love for God, whom we cannot see

17

yet who has created all visible goodness.

Such faithful service, in turn, is guided by the model of Jesus, my fourth point for ministry. We tell the story of Jesus day after day in the Church throughout the world because he, as our brother, really is the center of our connection with God. In him, God becomes humanly available and personal, just as faith becomes personally actual only in the local church. In Jesus, God meets us where and how we live. And that is why we tell his story. But the stories Jesus tells, the parables, take us into where and how he lives, into an experience of the gospel. And I want to say only one thing about that experience here. Jesus gave witness to the reign of God through parables manifesting the presence of God in strange places and in persons unexpected. The treasure hidden in the field, the outcast Samaritan who unexpectedly becomes "good," the imprisoned, naked, hungry persons who stand in for the Lord himself — these and other "stories" told us by Jesus guide our understanding of ministry. Perhaps they are saying we will spend our entire lives learning how close to us God has always been and how often we have overlooked his presence.

This brings us to the last characteristic of pastoral ministry. It is respectful and sensitive to those persons served. As the Rule of St. Benedict expresses it, "Receive each guest as Christ himself." For the service that loves is the ministry which affirms the one served. But in spite of this vital aspect of loving respect and acceptance, there will always be a certain "hardness" to the gospel. And we will all be tempted to escape from or to deny its challenge to us personally. Certainly we can say, "We are like Christ," but we must also add, "except in our sins." And Jesus' first preaching included the message,

"Repent." To comprehend this is not to take a "guilt trip" or to "lay one on others" but to know and deal with what is in us all. This is the realism of the gospel.

I have sought to guide my vision of the parish as a family of families according to realism on many levels. The vision seeks to answer a real need for the faith to reach into people's lives, homes, and families. The reality of sin also confronts us with new awareness of what happens when we exclude persons from our lives, homes, and families. When Jesus taught us to call God "Father," he said that, in principle, we all belong to the same family. What happens in practice, however, often follows the axiom, "blood is thicker than water." This can be used as an excuse to exclude or persecute others outside our blood ties of race, nation, ethnic group, or family. But our faith asserts that the spirit of Christ is more powerful than blood itself, that the spirit can bind person to person in a way blood cannot. In the spirit we become one body, one family, one people of God. This is our gift, our task, and my dream.

# II
# Listening
# as Ministry

## by Paul F. Wilczak, Ph.D.

*Paul F. Wilczak, Ph.D., is a staff member at the Center for Pastoral Life and Ministry of the Diocese of Kansas City-St. Joseph, Missouri. Contributing editor for MARRIAGE* and Family Living, *Dr. Wilczak's main professional interests are the pastoral care of families and the use of family systems theories in developing a theology of pastoral care.*

The woman had been talking to the pastor for ten minutes already. Her voice had become intense at times, as she spoke of long years of work and heavy personal responsibilities. Her voice took on a special edge when she mentioned Joe, her husband. The priest sat there motionless, stole a quick glance at the ceiling, and asked, "Have you discussed this problem with your husband?" She almost shouted her answer, "He doesn't talk! He just sits there." She hesitated for an instant, as if groping for the right words, and continued, "He's like a dog that comes in to eat and then lies down in a corner to snore. He's about that much companionship!" The pastor's brow furrowed as he leaned toward the woman. His mouth dropped open as if to speak and his image froze on the videotape monitor. I turned from the picture on the screen and asked the twenty parishioners who were watching, "What would you say to the lady now to let her know you understand what she is feeling?"

The audience was one of the groups enrolled in my six-week course entitled "Listening as Ministry." Among them were married and single persons, priests and religious. Their ages ranged from early twenties to past seventy. And they came to work on their listening as a means of enriching themselves and improving their ministry in their own families and to other families. We were exploring listening with the heart.

What is listening with the heart? It's the way *we listened* when we fell in love and came to the deep realization, "Yes, this is the one, the person with whom I want to share my life." It is the way we were listened to when, utterly alone and isolated by our problems, someone came along and said, "You seem to be having a tough time. Feel like talking?" And we did. Remember how great our relief was as we experienced the warm presence of another person's gift of understanding? This is heart-to-heart listening. It is characteristic of families who demonstrate their love in many little but significant ways. And it is also a mark of that extended Christian family called the People of God, the people who unite in worshiping and in Christian living.

Since much of my work at the Center for Pastoral Life and Ministry is devoted to helping the people of the Diocese of Kansas City-St. Joseph, Missouri, deepen their capacities for heart-to-heart encounter, I would like to comment on that work. I hope this will help others see how important listening is for extending and enriching the family of God present in local churches. I'll begin with what listening with the heart means, and then go on to the challenge it involves and its relevance as a ministry.

23

## Listening with the Heart

Let's consider listening first before we go on to the heart's role in the process. It is quite obvious that by listening I mean something more than just *hearing*. Hearing can mean mere sensitivity to sound, the healthy functioning of the organs of hearing. When I say *listening*, I mean giving my full attention to hearing someone. I include in listening the other senses, especially sight and touch. We could even speak of listening with the eyes or with the whole body. This is so because the specific sense is less important than the function of establishing contact with another person.

However, it is the "heart"—our total emotional response—that integrates these various perceptions into full, personal contact, and this is what is needed today. We can listen with our heads. We can comprehend the thought content of a person's message and systematically analyze what is communicated. This is cognitive empathy and can be readily learned. But cognitive empathy has severe limitations. It misses the dimension of meaning that goes beyond what is explicitly said. It overlooks the feelings and experiences usually conveyed without words. These other messages come from the heart, the center of a person's experience.

Listening to and with the heart is neither so readily taught nor so easily learned. Such listening aims at emotional empathy and even at comprehensive interpersonal resonance in so far as this is possible. In cognitive empathy, words have paramount importance. In emotional and comprehensive personal empathy, images and actions are more significant than words. The attention is not so much on *what* is said but *how*, that is, on *process* more than content. To express the impact of listening with the

24

heart, I like to use the illustration of one vibrating tuning fork setting another into sympathetic vibration. Our whole being vibrates with the message we receive when we take it to heart. But what takes place with people is much more complex than what happens with tuning forks. The fork has no say about its reaction to the sound waves. We do. In fact, we must intentionally take the message to heart in order to listen with full personal empathy. *We must become attuned* to the full import of messages on many levels to listen empathetically. And this takes work.

## The Challenge of Listening

Listening with the heart, from the core of our personal reality, is a *major challenge*. The task is very difficult, yet also necessary for human growth and development. A careful empirical study (S. Minuchin and others, *Families of the Slums,* 1967) has documented that multi-problem families are groups of people who do not listen to one another. There is characteristically hostile competition and delinquency within such families which spills out into the society. This often leads to the courts, to juvenile homes, or even to prison. But conflicts with the law are only outer manifestations of pervasive, unresolved conflicts within the families themselves. Public authorities are given as little respect as family members are. Within the multi-problem family with a delinquent member, the problems are maintained and deepened by a lack of listening. It has been discovered that in such families no one expects to be heard. These are noisy families in which people are used to tuning each other out. Or, if on occasion people are heard, they do not expect a response. There is no experience of making contact, of counting as a

25

person, or of making a significant impression. If there is some response, it is not usually relevant. Rather than connect with the other person's message, the one addressed indicates disregard for it and changes the subject.

Such a "response" I would prefer to call something else — a *reaction,* not a response. In the "listening" course, I use a videotape of a marriage counseling session to demonstrate how reactions work against listening responses. This is an important distinction because there can be no effective listening when people are merely reacting. The dominance of reactions reduces the very possibility of making listening responses.

Let me relate what I mean. In the tape, the marriage counselor directs the husband to describe to his wife what his feelings are "right now" about their relationship. The husband looks at the wife and says, "I don't think you understand at all how I feel. I don't like what's going on at home. It's a drag!" His wife reacts with the words, "I don't think I care how you feel. So you feel rotten! So what?" Neither was listening to the other, only reacting. The husband used a *fight* reaction of blaming; the wife, a *flight* reaction of "I don't care!" Both were protecting themselves rather than working on better mutual understanding. In brief, reacting is primarily to protect the self, while responding transcends reactions into mutual affirmation and listening.

## Listening as Ministry

At the Center, the "listening" course I teach is designed to train people in listening with the heart as a ministry within the local churches. The course has been offered for over a year and has proven to be a significant development in pastoral training. "Listening as Ministry" deals with skills which span the entire six areas of family ministry presented in the American Catholic bishops' *Plan of Pastoral Action for Family Ministry*. Included in the offering and carefully studied are examples of ministry to single persons, to married couples, to parents, to families with children of different ages, to "hurting" families, and to leaders in these ministries. A basic orientation to listening skills appropriate to each of these six areas is established and readied for further development in other Center offerings. At this time well over three hundred persons have been trained in "Listening as Ministry" through the Center for Pastoral Life and Ministry. They have been people with a wide variety of backgrounds and from both urban and rural churches. The participants have evaluated the course in writing, and their evaluations have been overwhelmingly positive.

What our people describe as most helpful to them are skills in the process of "active listening." These skills are presented and discussed in terms of theology and psychology, and participants read Thomas Gordon's *Parent Effectiveness Training* on "active listening." But the words shape into real interpersonal meanings with the close study of visual and auditory images on videotape and with the action of participants in role playing in the class and practicing the learned skills at home. Participants are guided in their understanding of basic skills and their application to family situations of increasing complexity. In six weeks they progress from listening to a college freshman who experiences the Mass as meaningless to listening to a family with two teenagers who have school problems. As the scope of listening is expanded to greater breadth and complexity, the store of meaning and skills is enriched.

27

But we are not concerned with listening as "social work" or as "counseling." Therefore, "Listening as Ministry" emphasizes a way to witness to the gospel by enacting its meaning or to announce the "good news" by making it happen. Very briefly stated, this mode of witness amounts to five things. Let us take a look at each.

• First, listening symbolizes God's presence. The minister who listens gives attention to the other out of a personal faith. The minister's own faith that he or she is listened to by God who understands his or her feelings, in a sense, allows God's concerned listening to be realized and sensed by others through the individual's ministry. This is an intricate theological point which cannot be expanded here. But the minister's own living faith is clearly stressed as the foundation for this mode of ministry.

• Next, listening enacts loving care. A ministerial listener must care enough to bother to listen. This is a form of love, and people who cannot bother to listen cannot love those they meet. An experience of ministerial listening renders the assertion, "God is love," more credible.

• Third, listening makes possible, for the persons in dialog, good communication—an achievement of *union with*. The most radical aspect of this binding together is that it gives us an actual experience of the union of all persons in the fatherhood of God. To listen to another is to affirm that person as a fellow member of God's family.

• And this brings up the fourth point about listening with the heart. Through listening there is *entry into another person's world* and its experiential qualities. Listening implies commitment, being sent with another person on a journey into his or her world. In this way, listening is comparable to the incarnation in which the Lord himself entered into our world and experienced its contours, thereby unveiling their patterns. In this analogy, listening as ministry becomes an imitation of Christ.

• The fifth point would quite logically go to "bearing one another's burdens and so fulfilling the law of Christ" (Gal 6:2) — being "unable" to walk away thinking, "I'm going to avoid her. What a downer! Why doesn't she get over it and not bother people with her troubles?" The person who serves by listening will not run out, but will enter the valley of darkness and sorrow with the other person. The minister does this, however, not because it feels comfortable but in spite of uncomfortable and anxious feelings.

It is not our discomforts and fears that cut us off from other people and from ourselves. It is our desire to live without such upsetting experiences and our attempts to avoid these unpleasant encounters. But human life includes traveling the gamut of experiences and feelings. And more important, our Christian calling expressed in the words, "Come, follow me," also includes the invitation, "Take up the cross." For as the Epistle to the Hebrews notes, "Since he himself has passed through the test of suffering, he is able to help those who are meeting their test now" (2:18). And here we can see the core of listening with the heart: it is to serve others by letting them touch what is in our own hearts and to surmount pain and sorrow by joining them in compassion. In this we shall reveal that we are his followers.

# III
# Family Ministry: The Elderly

by Dr. Margot Hover, D.Min.

*Formerly director of programs in Family Ministry for the Center for Pastoral Life and Ministry, Diocese of Kansas City-St. Joseph, Dr. Margot Hover is co-founder of Full Circle, a consulting service for parishes, schools, businesses, and civic groups. She is the author of five books and several hundred magazine articles.*

*"For years, I've seen good people undertake work for the church without the training and the support they've needed. They've gotten discouraged. The Center's job will be to prepare them to make a solid contribution and to find satisfaction in the ministry they've chosen."*

With these words, Bishop John Sullivan of the Roman Catholic Diocese of Kansas City-St. Joseph, Missouri, launched the Center for Pastoral Life and Ministry. The goal of the Center is to aid in identifying ministerial needs within specific parishes and to help train parishioners to minister to those needs.

Very quickly we were in business. The staff of Visitation Parish in Kansas City called on us to work with them in serving their large elderly population. Some services such as bus rides to Sunday Mass were already provided, and in general, these people were able to obtain other "survival" services. The real issue was their isolation. Most lived alone. Their children and other relatives were scattered, and contact with family was limited at best.

As a representative of the Center, I arranged a meeting in October with the pastor, Rev. Richard Carney, and the permanent deacon coordinating the program, Rev. Mr. George Kopp. Brother Larry Horn, who regularly visits the elderly of the parish, and Dr. Paul Wilczak of the Center staff also attended. At that first planning session, Paul (Dr. Wilczak) and I listened to the vision and concerns of the parish staff. They wanted to foster greater responsiveness from the parish families to the elderly within the parish, and they wanted to provide an opportunity for younger members of those parish families to experience the richness of a relationship with people who had lived a long life.

On the other hand, the staff was wary of alienating the elderly by any approach that would cast them in the role of helpless recipients. They were unsure of how to initiate contacts with the elderly people, afraid that any mention of their involvement in a "program" would evoke apprehension. They wanted to safeguard the independence and privacy of the elderly participants. Although it was clear that those families giving service would find their own lives enriched in turn, the staff was unsure as to how this would happen. They dreamed that the participants eventually would take leadership roles in the continuation of the project so that more families could be involved and trained for similar service.

Paul and I, too, had our concerns. We wanted the families involved to be well trained in skills directly related to their communication with the elderly. But their ability to communicate within their own households also could not be neglected. We wanted

33

them to be able to set limits on their involvement so that they would want to continue their ministry rather than "burn out" at some crucial moment along the way. And finally, we wanted them to be able to integrate their ministry with their understanding of Christian life, membership in the community of faith, and prayer.

Also, I felt that it was particularly important to involve all of the people participating in this family ministry to the elderly in various aspects of the training program. All—parents, children, and elderly— would need to learn a few new things. For a number of years, I had successfully conducted workshops for families where parents and their children all learned and practiced skills in communication, and I was convinced of the value of this approach.

Finally, we were all aware that the program might attract compulsive "do-gooders," more intent on their own contributions than aware of the real needs of their elderly "partners." (Partner was the term used for the elderly person participating in the program.) In other words, both parish and Center staffs were eager to promote sensitivity to people, at every level and in every way possible.

As we talked, a structure for the training program emerged. George Kopp had already recruited ten families who would be matched with ten elderly parishioners. He had spent several evenings with each family to make sure that the matter was discussed with children as well as with adults, and that all were aware of the time demands their commitment would involve. Each family knew that they would be trained for their ministry, and that the parish would provide ongoing staff support.

With this in mind, Paul and I formulated the following goals for our work with the families:

1. We wanted to provide all of the family members with opportunities to talk about their feelings regarding this new venture. What did it mean? What might it involve?

2. We wanted to help the parents and children alike to clarify, practice, and feel confident about the skills they would use in this ministry.

3. We hoped to assist the families in reflecting and praying with the parish staff as they progressed together in this common venture. They would all be mapping out new ways to show Christian concern and love. We wanted to help them celebrate the milestones on their journey.

4. To confirm and consolidate all of the above, we wanted to help all participants affirm, support, and challenge one another in their ministerial work and commitment.

In addition to these four goals, Paul and I also offered to provide supervision to the families as needed and to work with the parish staff to insure the continuation of the program in the years to come.

To accomplish these goals, we asked that Wednesday evenings from December through February be set aside for the training program. The parents of the host families attended each session; their children, regardless of age, were invited to four sessions, and their teenage children came to two more meetings with them. We planned for the elderly partners to attend four of the sessions. However, because of severe winter weather and other factors, this was not possible. While some of the elderly might have been shy about joining the group at the training sessions, others spoke with pride about being chosen to participate in the program. My hunch is that they would have enjoyed coming to the sessions with the families; perhaps they will be included in subsequent programs.

Each of the meetings included a brief prayer service. We wanted to provide an opportunity for the participants to consider and then voice their own views of the religious dimension of their work in the program. At the same time, we thought it would be helpful to offer the families some examples of shared family prayer that could be used later on in their own home.

And so we began. At the first meeting, all of us — participating parents, parish staff, and Center resource people — were introduced to each other. The parish staff reviewed the steps taken so far, and Paul and I presented an overview of the training program. We were both unprepared for the reaction of the group. Most guessed that their contributions to their elderly partners would consist primarily of such services as providing transportation and household repairs; the value of "listening skills" was unclear to them. Others felt that they were being forced to move too rapidly; what if their partner would be reluctant to join the project? There was a good deal of trepidation; it was a tribute to the goodwill and trust generated by the parish staff that all of the host families — children and parents — came to the next meeting.

At the second session, we suggested some ways of making the initial contact with the partners. All had received a preliminary call from one of the staff members, and now we asked the families to make three contacts during the month before our next meeting, after the Christmas holidays.

Then, we used roleplay and discussion of scripts that we provided to help the families to think about the specific hopes they had and possible limits for their involvement. At the conclusion of the discussion, we asked each parish staff member to anoint the hands of the parents as they sat with their children. They, in turn, anointed their children as we all recalled the privilege and the dedication required of Christians called to minister to one another.

At the third meeting, after Christmas, we asked the families to formulate a list of hopes they had for their relationship with their partners. Nearly all of the families had spent some time with their partner over the holidays. Some hoped for more general things such as a "chance to grow" or "an opportunity to share " Others were more specific. One father said, "I hope my children get a sense of history and living tradition from talking with a person who has experienced a long life."

One month later, we asked the families to list the gifts of time, material support, service, and spirit which they had given and received from their partner. This time, the lists were considerably longer and more detailed. One family recognized the gift of their partner's time, as well as the maps she had given the children, for example. Another family realized how much they enjoyed a project that they could work on as a family. Thus, even at the beginning, it was clear that the relationship involved both giving and receiving on both sides.

During the next two weeks, Paul and I worked with the parents and their teenagers to provide some theory and much practice in "active" listening. The younger generation relished the experience of learning along with their parents. Initially, the parents commented that this kind of listening was something they did without thinking, as a matter of course. As we worked, they came to see why so many of their automatic responses — moralizing, distracting, giving advice, for example — were not as helpful as reflecting the feelings they heard. The outcome of these sessions was a deepened respect for the value of good listening and an awareness of the importance of eye contact and body language in any communication.

In early February, two months into the program, Paul and I met with the parents alone to review skills and answer questions. Since the second session, we had met in a large hall, but on this evening, we returned to the small study where we had come together for the first time. Paul and I listened while the couples summarized what they had experienced and learned thus far. As the people related their growing satisfaction with the program, we remembered the reservations and anxieties of the first meeting. "We always did things like getting our partner's mail and sweeping the sidewalks, but this time *we* had to make the overture instead of being asked. We wouldn't have taken that step alone," one couple related. Two families spoke of the joy they experienced when they were invited to visit their partners' homes. While they realized that it was good for the elderly to share their memories with them as friends, they and their children were also sincerely interested in hearing the stories and seeing the albums and accumulated keepsakes. One mother chuckled at the comfortable frankness of her seven year old, who went up to the widow they had "adopted" and said, "Gee, everything in this house is old, even you."

While they were aware that they could give service and alleviate loneliness and fear, the couples also found their own lives enriched. "I've begun to listen to my wife and the kids in a way that I never did before," said one father. One couple had to withdraw from the level of participation they had planned when one of their own elderly parents came to stay with them. They were direct and responsible about priorities. "I've learned that it's all right to meet the obligations I have at home now without feeling guilty because I'm not doing lots of things for other people," said the woman.

As Paul and I led the couples to reflect on their experience, they were able to point to two factors that contributed to their sense of satisfaction with the program First, they had gained a new appreciation of the need for specific skills for undertaking ministry. Several could recall the frustration of previous situations when they felt unqualified to successfully accomplish some service for the Church. At this point, they saw the need and rewards for performing this service skillfully.

Second, they knew that the support of the parish staff and of the rest of the group was important. As the end of our involvement drew near, they spoke of their determination to continue meeting at least occasionally to affirm each other and to celebrate what was taking place. The parish staff's inquiry about their participation in subsequent training programs for other families was met with enthusiasm.

At our last session together, we met with the adults to discuss the sacrament of the anointing of the sick. Having spoken so often of the giving and receiving done by both host families and partners, we now dealt with the role for which the elderly are anointed The person is blessed as death comes near, always unknown and sometimes painful and frightening. But further, people are anointed for the service of witnessing to us about the realizations that come with facing the end of this life. We suggested that the parish staff make the opportunity for the reception of this sacrament available during the month after the final session, preferably when each partner could be surrounded by the family members who had touched their lives in the program.

At the end of our three months of Wednesday evenings at Visitation Parish, Paul and I noticed that the people now spoke of their family involvement as ministry. Thus, what had earlier been seen in terms of "doing something for the widow down the street" came to be seen in the context of Christian care that was both given and received. At the Center for Pastoral Life and Ministry, we had defined ministry as "service rendered out of love, after the model of Jesus, with deep reverence for the participant's freedom, individuality, and growth." Here, we saw this in action. For this group of families and their elderly partners, Bishop Sullivan's dream had begun to come true.

# IV
# The Family
and Social Justice

by Susan Rakoczy, IHM

*Susan Rakoczy, IHM, has her Ph.D. in religion from Catholic University of America. She is a staff member at the Center for Pastoral Life and Ministry, Kansas City, Missouri, with special interests in spirituality and social justice.*

Words, like clothes, have fashions. Teens know this well as each year's slang is replaced by new "in" language. So, too, in the Christian community, certain words carry both the burden of much attention and use and the suspicion that there is more here than just a "catchword" or slogan.

Today two words of this type are "family" and "justice." "Family" has never been "out," of course, but with the focus of the Catholic Church in this country during the 1980s being placed on the family, the word has begun to carry much more weight than previously. "Family" begins to connote both a life-style of sharing and intimacy and the specific structures that enable this life to happen among people.

"Justice," especially "social justice," has assumed an important place in the contemporary Church since the 1960s. Its significance was heightened for Catholics when, at the Synod of 1971, their bishops declared it to be a "constitutive dimension of the preaching of the Gospel." Justice for them was not an optional "icing on the cake" of Christian life, but an essential part of Christian teaching.

In one sense, family is easy to deal with — we all have some familiarity with it, whether our experience now or in the past ever exemplified "a typical family" situation. But justice is harder to grasp. It has an abstract quality that is not dispelled when the evening news comes parading through our homes, graphic with situations of injustice. The more we know, it seems, about world and local and national situations, the more we seem paralyzed by the immensity of the situations in which justice is not yet done.

How can these two words, which the Spirit speaks to the Christian community today, be brought together? We know that the family must reach out to embrace the world and do justice, but how do we begin and how do we avoid the fear caused by the suspicion that, despite our best efforts, nothing changes?

Sometimes a detour is, in the end, a more direct route than the main road we had planned on taking. I would like to suggest that rather than first dealing with "social justice" as a family responsibility, we reflect on "social conversion" as the basis for doing justice.

"Social conversion" brings the concept of "justice" from the abstract to the concrete by beginning right where we are today. All conversions are passages from death to life; social conversion is the passage from the "old way" of seeing the world from our own little individual perspective to a wider vision which expands our minds and hearts to include the whole world. We begin to feel and experience that

43

we are truly sisters and brothers to everyone in our neighborhood, our parish, our city, our country, and our world. And, as sisters and brothers, there is no one whose life and concerns are somehow not ours also. In the words of St. Paul, we are truly "members of one another" (1 Cor 12:12), and this experience becomes the prime focus of the way we make decisions, live our lives, and relate to one another.

"Social conversion" is the basic Christian vision of how people are bonded together. The "word" may be new, but the reality pointed to has long been the heart of Christian preaching and life.

The baptismal gift has two dimensions: personal and communal. As individuals, we are made a new creation in Christ Jesus and we become part of a community of believers. We are called to community life, not to a rugged individualism. However, our communal life is generally quite weak and we seldom experience the depth and power of what has already been given to us.

The reasons for this are easy enough to see in our church and our society. Though our faith is communal, our formation as Christians is usually quite individual. "My spiritual life," "my salvation," "my prayer life" has become the language of our experience.

But our society also shouts a siren message that, in the end, you had better look out only for yourself because no one else will bother. Evidences of this are all around us. The seventies were variously called the "Me" or the "Me First" generation. Advertising and the media focus on building on the natural selfishness of which we all have more than enough, to exalt it as the prime value of our lives. "Aren't *you* worth it?" the ads croon to us.

The ever-galloping materialism of this century has also done its damage to us by insisting that it is what you have that counts, not who you are. The emphasis on acquisition of "more" and "better" builds effective barriers between people. "The rich" and "the poor" become abstract groups based on income and possessions (or their lack) and we, who have some things (although not as many as we would wish), congratulate ourselves on our good fortune, forgetting that the "poor" are flesh and blood like ourselves.

The American value of time-consciousness further limits the vision we have of the world as our family. Time has become a commodity to be hoarded — not an environment of availability to be shared. We all plead that "we have no time," and, at the same time, use the time we have to build bigger walls around our families by isolating ourselves in our houses, furnished with every diversion to keep the world out and people isolated from one another. If one television set, watched by the whole family together, can lead to a passive isolation, let us reflect on what three or four TVs in a household do both to the sense of community and the use of family time. The old saying, "If you want something done, ask a busy person — no one else has any time" rings even truer today as our individual use of time becomes ever more precious and our vision of how to use that time narrows.

Lastly, the increase of crime in the last 15 years has helped us to absorb the message that "the stranger is the enemy." We have widened our fear-threshold to embrace not only those who might do us harm, but also all who are strangers to our world. Sameness of thought and life-style becomes a prime value when "differentness" becomes a threat. Our life-style becomes less and less open to the marginal persons of our society, those who have little to contribute by their productivity, because we are so intent on proving who we are by what we have and what we do.

How different is the gospel vision! It becomes easier to see year by year that the gospel and our commitment to Christ Jesus call us to a radical counter-cultural life-style and world view. Whether we use the term "social conversion" or not, reflection on the teaching of the gospel shows us that this wider vision is at the heart of our lives as Christians.

Let us look at several gospel incidents with an eye to see what they tell us about social relationships. The story of Martha and Mary (Luke 10:38-42) has often been used by preachers to dichotomize the "active" from the "contemplative" life and to exalt the latter. But more is entwined in that story than two ways of life. It is most essentially about hospitality. Martha and Mary welcomed Jesus into their home and, because Jesus traveled with his friends, they surely also would have been welcomed. It was a privilege for these two women to have their friend and famous rabbi enter their home — no wonder there was much commotion and bustling about. But Jesus' words to Martha — you are anxious about many things when only one is needed — is not a call to contemplative prayer, but a reminder that hospitality is first welcoming persons as persons and then serving them in concrete ways.

Opening our home to people who are not totally known to us (After all, in some ways we are all strangers to one another.) is primarily creating a setting where we meet as persons. It is not what we serve for dinner or how it is served that matters. It is the attention we give to this guest who is now friend that should shape our practice of hospitality. As this person becomes part of our lives, the walls between us fall and we see each other no longer in "justice categories" — the old, the sick, the stranger, the refugee, the welfare family — but as sisters and brothers.

Matthew's familiar depiction of the final judgment as based on service to those in need forms another building block of the foundation for social conversion. We generally feel confident that we will respond to expressed needs ("Just let me know what you want and I'll do it.") but we all frequently close our eyes to that which is beyond our immediate vision. The parable of the judgment reminds us that we need not wait to be asked to do good nor to be told that this "is the Christian thing" to do. The experience of our solidarity together — as all human beings loved by God — should be more than enough motivation for us to stretch our hands, hearts, and resources outward to those in need.

The gospels describe several occasions when Jesus fed the multitude who had just a few loaves and fishes (Mark 6:30-44, John 6:1-14). Two things happened in those miracles — the bread and fishes were multiplied to feed the crowd and a person's standard of what is "enough for me" dropped as each shared what had been given rather than earned.

Economists and social scientists are insisting that the American economy is in a stage of contraction and that we all will have to learn to live with less. What tragedy will result if we continue to refuse to share the remaining resources and gifts we already have! As a "simple life-style" no longer becomes an option for "radical Christians" but the norm of all of our lives, we will cause great scandal if we refuse to accept the economic limitations imposed upon us as opportunities to demonstrate that, however little we may have, it must be shared.

Saying a thing and doing it are two distinct activities. Understanding "social conversion" as the basis for doing justice as Christians helps us little without practical guidance on how to live this gift that is already ours, but is so little experienced.

In the family, parents are the first teachers of their children. "Action on behalf of justice," concrete love in action, will happen in a family first, to the degree that the parents carefully examine their values and what they are teaching their children. How wide is their vision? Does the world stop at the front door — is the family a safe refuge from the world and its problems? It would be well for parents to sit down and list for two weeks or so, 1) the topics of dinner-table conversations, 2) the kinds and number of family activities, 3) the decisions about spending money on things/persons outside the family circle, 4) attitudes toward each others' friends, and 5) prejudiced comments about others of different races, ethnic backgrounds, economic levels.

"Doing justice," which is the fruit of social conversion, can happen only in and through a family when all agree that this is their vision. Parents and children must become "co-decision makers for justice."

The Buddhist concept of "mindfulness" can be helpful to us here. This orientation to life concentrates on what is happening to me right now, with the exclusion of everything else. For example, when I am washing dishes, I am washing dishes, not planning my next forty activities. This type of "consciousness" can be especially valuable when families (and individuals in the families) make decisions about the use of money and family resources. We need to ask ourselves: 1) Who says we need this thing? 2) If we don't buy it, what will happen? 3) If we truly need it, how and where shall we buy it? 4) Is there anything in the way we purchase it that can show our solidarity with the poor and oppressed of our world? For example, at birthday or Christmastime, rather than buying expensive commercial gifts, the same love can be expressed by making a gift or buying crafted articles. The stress on "mindfulness" is knowing why you are doing what you are doing, and how it will affect others.

The horizons for the children need to be constantly widened in the family. American family life has had a tendency to exalt children and build the family structure around them. This orientation tends to increase children's sense of "me-firstness" and limit their acceptance of people outside of themselves.

If a family consciously makes hospitality part of its life together, the children will begin to see their family as a place where others — diverse and rich in gifts — are made welcome. "The world is already too much with us" from TV news — we know the abstract problems. Our world needs to be made concrete in its persons. Thus the family home should be a place not only where the family relates and the parents' and children's friends are made welcome and become friends with all the members of the family, but where the "marginal people" of our society also find welcome. This can be as simple as "adopting" an older person in the neighborhood to be part of the family circle — especially if the grandparents live in other parts of the country and the children have little contact with an aging person. Persons of different cultures and backgrounds can be part of the family — foreign exchange students, the refugee family your parish is helping — the possibilities are endless.

More than simply inviting the stranger into the household, the family must go beyond itself in action. Parents and children must be constantly creative to keep the windows of the family home open outward. Activities such as working at a Catholic Worker house, visiting the aged in nursing homes, working on parish social justice projects, collecting for UNICEF at Halloween, using part of the family budget for charities that all decide upon, having simple meals of bread and soup in Lent and Advent and sharing the money saved from a "regular" meal with a group like Bread for the World or Oxfam, getting acquainted with the projects in your area that are funded by the Campaign for Human Development, or giving some of the produce from the family garden to the poor can increase our solidarity with the poor and marginal persons of our society. Our aim is not simply to "speak the truth in love" but to experience the truth that we are all one in Christ in ways that are as real as our hands and feet.

As our vision widens, as our solidarity with our sisters and brothers across our city and world grows, as strangers become friends we have newly made, social justice will lose its feeling of being an impossible ideal to achieve. Rather, our connectedness with our fellow human beings in Christ Jesus will necessarily impel us to put our bodies, bank accounts, and values on the line toward creating a world where "there shall be no more death or mourning, crying out or pain, for the former world has passed away" (Rev 21:4). This vision is not an idle dream; it is a look into a future that is shaped by our love, and where the doing of justice has made us all experience the reality of family in God.

# V
# The Family: Journey of Initiation and Conversion

by Maureen Kelly

*Maureen Kelly is Program Coordinator for the Center for Pastoral Life and Ministry, Diocese of Kansas City-St. Joseph, Missouri. She has an M.A. in theology and has also done graduate work in psychology and counseling. Ms. Kelly was a Diocesan Director of Religious Education.*

"Mommy, who made me?" asks the young child and Mother answers, "God made you." There are other questions too, such as: "Is there ice cream in heaven?" Or the question my nephew, Michael, asked his father after listening to his dad's account of the story of Abraham and Isaac: "But Daddy, how could God do such a thing?" As our children grow, their questions change into "Why do we have to go to church?" Sometimes we hear the statement "I didn't ask to be baptized" and many families experience their young adults "leaving the church" or "losing their faith."

In the past twenty-five years (since I was in the eighth grade) in the American Catholic Church there have been tremendous changes in the way we educate persons to faith. Indoctrination and rote learning, so prevalent in my growing-up years, are losing their force. The generation of grandparents who were so wise and sure about God and heaven and the Church, and where we were all going, has been replaced by a generation which has often experienced the rug being pulled out from under them.

My own mother, a woman who told many stories about God and faith to her own children, hesitates when her grandchildren ask their questions today. She often remarks: "With all the changes today, I'm just not sure what's right anymore." The family piety that was so much a part of our Irish Catholic heritage is not evident as such in my brothers' families. Their sons are not struggling with learning the Latin altar boy responses nor are their daughters rushing off to the Miraculous Medal Novena on Monday nights. When someone loses something the immediate response is not, "Pray to St. Anthony" but, "Where were you when you had it last?" The religion books my nieces and nephews bring home from Catholic school and CCD classes are a far cry from our own Baltimore Catechisms and speak a language sometimes foreign to our generation. Things have changed and a question is being asked today by parents that was not a question for their parents: "Will our children have faith?"

As a single laywoman in the Catholic Church, my ministry revolves around teaching theology and dealing with religious educators. It is from within that milieu that I share these thoughts with you. My answer to the question, "Will our children have faith?" is: It all depends.

What I have come to realize is that it does not depend on having the right answers; it does not depend on novenas; it does not depend on whether we have Catholic schools or CCD programs. It does not depend on the textbooks our children use. What does it depend on?

1) It all depends on what we mean by faith. 2) It all depends on how we help our children recognize God in our midst. (Which, of course, depends on whether we recognize him ourselves.) 3) It all depends on what environments our children grow up in.

When we ask the question about faith, it is necessary to ask what we mean by faith. In general, faith is loyalty to something or someone. We all have faith in something or someone. We are loyal — loyal to our spouse, loyal to our job, loyal to our country. Another way of putting it is that most of us *entrust* ourselves to some reality at the center of our loyalties which holds us together when it seems that our whole world may be falling apart.

Abraham is called the Father of Believers. His most enduring trait was his loyalty to Yahweh. Yahweh promised. Abraham waited. Sometimes he suffered. He could not see how the promised was to occur but he remained faithful and so did God. He knew, implicitly perhaps, what kind of God he believed in: a caring God, a personal God, a God who was a rock no matter what — war, peace, sorrow, joy; in good times and bad times he was trustworthy.

In our Christian experience, God has shown himself to us as one of our own in the person of Jesus and in his promise to remain with us always. The trust in God's promise and presence, particularly in the person of Jesus, is what we call faith.

What Christian faith gives us is an ordered, consistent way of looking at the world. We often use the phrase, "in the light of faith." This gives us some idea of the ultimate purpose of Christian faith: to enlighten us. Because we are a Christian people, we see differently the meaning of life. Both personally and communally we are convinced that because

Jesus Christ lived, died, and rose, death has been overcome. Faith allows us to live in hope not only for ourselves, in the small deaths and resurrections we experience, but also for the whole of creation. Faith is a gift but it is also a response. It enables us to live with ambiguity and to set forth on the journey of life as Abraham did.

There are several theories of faith development prominent in the catechetical field today. James Fowler's[1] and John Westerhoff's[2] are probably the two most espoused by contemporary religious educators. It is not my task here to explain or develop them but merely to cite them for those who might be interested and to bring attention to the fact that they both see the "faithful" as moving from a secure faith, or primitive faith in other people's faith, through a stage of tension and searching, seen very often in adolescents, to a faith of meaning that is integrated into and chosen by a person.

It seems then, that as parents and teachers, we must make a distinction between faith and religion. Faith is dynamic and it is ultimate. Religion is faith's expression. Once we make that distinction, we begin to realize that what is of primary concern is the development of faith. Religion, that is, our institutions, our creeds, our rituals, will, as it always has, develop out of faith. In partial answer to our question: Our children will not necessarily have faith if we think our work is accomplished by teaching them about Roman Catholicism, Lutheranism, or any other institutionalized "faith." That is not to negate the role of tradition or the place of a traditioning

---

[1] *Alfred McBride, "Spiritual Education: Fowler's Stages of Faith,"* Momentum *(May 1975), pp. 22-25.*

[2] *John Westerhoff,* Will Our Children Have Faith? *(New York: Seabury, 1976).*

community in the development of our faith or the faith of our children.

Using the image of faith as a journey, we see ourselves as a pilgrim people, the nomads of the Exodus experience. This journey to liberation entails hardship at times. It is a journey that cannot be made alone, rather it is done in community. Now, as then, individuals develop their faith by listening to the stories (traditioning) that others tell them about Yahweh and discerning his presence in their own here and now experience. It is recognition of this God among us and our sharing it that is the foundation of faith and conversion in our own lives and the lives of our children.

To articulate this God experience in their lives is often difficult for people. Their exclusive or excessive involvement in who made them and why ("God — to show forth his goodness") blunts their concern with such questions as: What kind of a person am I because God made me? Until people reverse their questions, their experience of fragility and sin is very often stronger than their experience of goodness and the presence of the Lord in their lives.

If our children are to have faith, it is necessary that the significant adults in their lives are able to talk with them and not at them about who God is, what difference Jesus makes, and why going to church is important for them. "Talking with" as opposed to "talking to" says a lot about what we mean by "ministering God's presence to one another." We are all on this journey of faith together. None of us has arrived and no matter how old we are or how much religion we have learned, none of us has all the answers.

Catechesis, or religious education, is one way of ministering God's presence and word. If our chil-

dren are to have faith, our fundamental mode of catechesis has to create a balance between nurture and conversion. For us to center on conversion, to call ourselves a people radically rooted in and celebrating the dying and rising of Jesus, says we are about more than being a religion or teaching a religion. It says we are about being a faithful people.

When we concentrate on religion in the narrow sense we tend to keep our basic pray, pay, and obey categories, and we keep our school models and multiply formal programs. We keep playing around with ages for this and ages for that and schedule and organize everything. To accept the gift of faith, which is offered so gratuitously to us, means we have to leap. One does not leap by hanging on.

I feel that what we have been called to recently, in my own Roman Catholic faith community, is a rekindling of faith. This seems obvious to me in the documents of Vatican II and, I think, even more in the renewal of our rituals. There has been, in the past, an imbalance of nurture and conversion in the method and context of our catechesis. In some instances, relying only on nurture, we have taken our baptized pagans and made them educated atheists. We have spent a lot of money and some of our best people preparing children for solemn apostasy.

Nurture makes possible incorporation. We nurture people into institutional religion but not mature faith. There is certainly a need for nurture. It is the ground of faith development. Yet our mode of catechesis ultimately has to be one where persons are helped and encouraged toward radical conversion. This requires a catechetical context that incorporates experience, time for reflection and insight, and opportunity to experiment and reflect on alternatives, to judge, and then to decide. It involves a context where persons are more important than things.

No one can teach or give faith; however, we do act and live in faith with one another. Faith development is a process by which people are nurtured in a community's faith and then internalize it and make it their own. The making of faith one's own results in transformation. Being respectful of this process in peoples' lives involves seeing the community as one which is on its way, one where individual and corporate stories are shared, one where exploring and having the questions is more important than having all the answers. It is the element of conversion that leads to mystery and catches us in God's surprise and the reality of the experience of being part of the parable of the Word made flesh. To stay in a mode of catechesis that is only nurturing (and we can do this with adults too) is to rob ourselves of the sense of being a pilgrim community.

To focus on nurturing alone results in a way of life and liturgy that is turned in on ourselves where we live. It says "Bless us," rather than, "Let us give praise to what God is realizing in us." It also is a barrier to our joining in the universal Church's celebration of its conversion as community. A catechetical context based solely on nurture sees the pilgrim community committed to the value of uniformity rather than to the event we are realizing as Church; and that is the dying and rising of Jesus and the coming of the Kingdom. It is this mode of catechesis that reduces our celebration of the Eucharist to two themes nourishment and fellowship meal. Lucien Deiss[3] puts it this way:

> "When a community no longer celebrates Christ's sacrifice or enters into it (which is what conversion is about) they end up assembling merely to eat together among friends. Sometimes finding there is no true fellowship or love on the community level they even omit the fellowship meal, since it no longer expresses anything. Then the erosion of the community's sacrificial sense stops by itself simply because there is no more community at all."

Catechesis occurs in a context. The most real and viable context for catechesis of our children today or always is family. Family is where we learn what kind of persons we are because God made us

---

[3]*Lucien Deiss*, It's the Lord's Supper, *(New York: Paulist Press, 1976), p. 38.*

and family is where we experience God's basic self revelation, that is: a God who both calls and confronts. Family is where we develop our capacity to be open to that revelation because that is where we develop our capacity to be open to the events of human life. There are other elements in the development of faith but these are probably the most fundamental.

Going back to my original scenario, I am often asked: "But if you did not have all that Irish Catholic background and all that Baltimore Catechism training, would you be where you are today?" Perhaps not. However, I suspect it wasn't the novenas for me or the learning of Latin for my brothers. At some point in the lives of the five of us and also in the lives of my parents there was a point of "leaving the Church" and talk of a "faith lost." In each instance, we "came back" a little more mature, less secure, and more rooted in the mystery of faith.

I do not fear for the faith of my nephews and nieces either because I see in their families what existed in ours, and that is the daily concrete experience of the sacrament of marriage: the basic affirmation of gifts and talents of each member of the family; the freedom to express one's sinfulness and be forgiven and reconciled; the freedom to make decisions, as difficult as that might be for the adults to watch; and the capacity to live with those decisions or change them as the case may be. Coupled with this is the ease with which their parents relate these experiences to talk about God. I don't hear the pat answers we learned as children. What I hear is adults, who have come to a deeper faith in and love of God and the Church, sharing that with their children in a language that is understandable and with an attitude that is grace-full and open.

# Questions for Reflection
and Discussion

# My Vision of the Parish
## as a Family of Families
(See pp. 11-19.)

A Roman Catholic bishop speaks his mind on the meaning and value of the local church and how to best activate its members to a full measure of the Christian life.

1. Bishop Sullivan lays great stress on the importance of Christian witness. What does this mean in your own life, particularly in your family life?

2. The local church should be a place of hospitality. Is that true for your own local church? Is it true for your own family? How is the message of hospitality best communicated in our world of strangers?

3. The author emphasizes local training. From your perspective, how can this best be done in your own local setting? What kind of training is available to you? Does your pastor or minister know your feelings in this matter? How might you share your views on this?

# Listening as Ministry
(See pp. 21-29.)

The ministry of listening involves listening to another person with uncommon awareness coupled with a reaching-out to his or her real situation.

1. Can you name experiences in your own life where you can say that you exercised "a ministry of listening"? How might these be related to the vitality of your marriage or family life?

2. Do you believe that it is difficult to really listen to another person? Why?

3. What do you see as the religious significance of listening? Which of the five theological dimensions of listening, listed by the author, spoke most to your own understanding?

# Family Ministry: The Elderly
(See pp. 31-40.)

Many elderly people live alone. They have been separated from their own families. Many younger families live apart from parents and grandparents. Programs can be developed to create new family arrangements, Christian extended families, to meet the needs these situations create.

1. Should the Church be involved in facilitating the kind of communal relationships described in this chapter? Why?

2. Was there anything in the program outlined in this chapter that you could apply to your own family? What about your local church or parish?

3. It is said that ministry always goes both ways — you cannot express it without receiving it. How is this illustrated in this chapter? Can you point to personal experiences where this has happened to you?

# The Family and Social Justice
(See pp. 41-52.)

Two themes have gained greater emphasis for Roman Catholics in recent years: family life and social justice. This chapter sketches the relationship between the two. It offers concrete suggestions as to how an awareness of justice may be developed within the family. It calls the family to consider its lifestyle and priorities in light of the needs of all persons.

1. In your view, is the family a community which contributes to the problem of injustice or its solution? Give your thoughts on both sides of the question.

2. How do the patterns of family life teach a sense of justice? How do you understand the concept of "social conversion" as it is described in the article? How has religion inhibited a sense of social awareness?

3. What is your understanding of Christian hospitality? Look at the kinds of people you invite into your home. What kind of message is preached by your practice?

4. What concrete steps can you take to bring your family to a wider sense of "family" and to meet the responsibilities which would stem from that expanded awareness?

# The Family: Journey of Initiation and Conversion
(See pp. 55-64.)

Religious education has been undergoing some rather fundamental shifts in recent years. Maureen Kelly places stress on the importance of religious conversion and the effect that such a conversion will have on the way religious questions are posed. The task of religious education should center on the family as the fundamental social group.

1. What do you understand as the difference between a conversion approach and a nurturing approach to religious education? What do you think of the article's comment that much of our religious education takes baptized pagans and makes them into educated atheists?

2. What kinds of loyalties does your family profess? How are they expressed?

3. Why does the family take on such an important role in religious education if conversion is understood as basic? How does the family show where God is active? How does the family point to God?

# Suggested Readings

Abbott, Walter, and Gallagher, Joseph. *The Documents of Vatican II*. New York: Herder and Herder, 1966.

It is startling to see how fresh these documents emerge upon rereading. Of special relevance to the model of the Church as an extended family are *Constitution on the Church* (sec. 13) and *Constitution on the Church in the Modern World* (secs. 27 and 32).

Alternatives Corporation. *Alternative Celebrations Catalogue*. Bloomington, IN: Alternatives, Inc. 1978.

This publication includes a wealth of suggestions on how to begin to simplify one's life-style and how to celebrate both religious and secular holidays in noncommercial ways. There is a study guide from the same organization, *Voluntary Simplicity,* by Eugenia Durland-Smith, that can be used in thinking through a simpler life-style for family living.

Brubaker, Timothy H., and Sneden, Lawrence E. "Aging in a Changing Family Context." *The Family Coordinator* 27.

This special issue provides an up-to-date, comprehensive review of significant theories, projects, and sociological patterns related to aging and the family.

Callahan, William, and Cardman, Francine, eds. *The Wind Is Rising*. Washington, D.C.: Quixote Center, 1978.

Reflections by Christians of various life-styles and commitments on how to integrate prayer and concern for justice in one's daily life.

Crosby Michael H., O.F.M. Cap. *Thy Will Be Done: Praying the Our Father as a Subversive Activity* Maryknoll, NY: Orbis Books, 1977.

Crosby presents this most famous prayer to us in an unfamiliar way: as a prayer that challenges our presuppositions about who God is and how we are to do his will, the work of justice, today.

Haughey, John C., ed. *The Faith that Does Justice*. New York: Paulist Press, 1977.

In these essays, a number of American theologians discuss the historical, theological, and pastoral bases of Christian action on behalf of justice in our world today.

Hellwig, Monika. *The Eucharist and the Hungers of the World*. New York: Paulist Press, 1976.

The Eucharist is strongly linked to human concerns and social justice. Hellwig maintains that celebration without action for justice is a distortion of the gospel.

Kerr, Kathleen B. "Issues in Aging . . . From a Family Perspective." *The Family* 7:3-10.

This excellent article in the journal of the Georgetown University Family Center is a thought-provoking consideration of families with aged members. It explains the implications of Murray Bowen's theory of family systems for issues in aging.

O'Brien, David, and Shannon, Thomas A. eds. *Renewing the Earth: Catholic Documents on Peace, Justice and Liberation.* New York: Doubleday, 1977.

A compilation of the basic church statements on social justice of the last ninety years.

Solnick, Robert L. ed. *Sexuality and Aging.* rev. ed. Los Angeles: University of Southern California Press, 1978.

This book deals sensitively with a neglected aspect of later life. Medical, physiological, and social service implications are clearly discussed.

Usdin, Gene, and Hofling, Charles K. eds. *Aging: The Process and the People.* New York: Brunner/Mazel, 1978.

This is an outstanding source of information from a psychiatric perspective. Included are chapters on the cultural context of aging, depression, and cognition. It includes a review of recent research.

Westerhoff, John H. *Will Our Children Have Faith?* New York: Seabury, 1976.

A fresh look at the question of developing adolescents' faith.